EVERYDAY

low carb

SLOW COOKER

30 DELICIOUS
LOW CARB SLOWCOOKER RECIPES
TO KICK-START WEIGHT LOSS

Disclaimer

Introduction

Low Carb Slow Cooker Cookbook introduces the low-carbohydrate diet to help you lose weight and take control of your life once more. The low-carbohydrate diet is unrivaled, leaving its proponents with a slim-waist and six pack abs. But how, precisely, does it work?

Let's look at the science. Essentially, carbohydrates are made up of glucose. Glucose is a sugar, and when it enters your body, it immediately lends itself to fueling your cells to do their everyday cell mechanisms. As you probably know, your cells are constantly working to keep you breathing, keep you moving, and keep you alive. And glucose is absolutely necessary in order to make that happen.

However, when you continually refuel yourself with glucose, your body has no need to look to other stored fat cells for fuel. Therefore, your body doesn't diminish its fat cell count; it continually works through the carbohydrates you fuel it with. You're making it easy on yourself, and you're doing your body no real favors. When you eat a low-carbohydrate diet, however, your body becomes confused. You are not lending it all the necessary glucose your cells require in order to work properly; therefore, your body must look to other sources. When you eat mostly fat and protein, the fat and protein have to undergo a process called ketosis. Your fat and protein molecules are transferred to glucose in the liver. Your body must work hard to do this, thus burning far more calories to digest these molecules than it usually does to digest carbohydrate foods.

Furthermore, when you don't fuel yourself with a carbohydrate-stocked diet, you won't unnecessarily impact your blood sugar levels. After you eat a rich carbohydrate meal, your blood sugar spikes unnecessarily; this boosts your insulin levels, as well. When your insulin and glucose levels fall once more, however, you're left craving sugary, carbohydrate-rich foods; the cycle will continue. However, when you regulate your carbohydrate intake, your body gets much better at regulating your appetite. Less carbohydrates means less insane sugar cravings.

Combining this scientifically proven low-carbohydrate diet with the slow cooker is essential genius for any person on-the-go. The slow cooker eliminates hours and hours of hard work at the end of the day. It brings healthful, flavorful options, and it fills your home with warmth and delightful smells. Each recipe in this book, outlined as either breakfast, pork, beef, chicken, chili, or soup-based, takes only a few minutes to toss together. Allow the slow cooker to do the rest while you continue on with your day.

Lose weight, save time, and keep yourself well. Bring endless flavor into your life, and rejuvenate yourself. Food is the ultimate comfort, the ultimate fuel, and your slow cooker eliminates its hassle once and for all!

Table of Contents

BREAKFAST LOW-CARBOHYDRATE
SLOW COOKER RECIPES

LAZY MORNING SAUSAGE AND BACON BREAKFAST CASSEROLE

Recipe Makes 8 Servings.
Nutritional Breakdown Per Serving: 428 calories, 4 grams net carbohydrates, 38 grams fat, 18 grams protein.

Ingredients:

1 pound cooked sausage
12 ounces crumbled bacon pieces
1 green bell pepper
1 yellow onion
1 ½ cups mushrooms
1 ½ cups spinach
½ cup feta cheese
2 cups Monterrey Jack cheese
1 cup heavy white cream
12 eggs
salt and pepper to taste

Directions:

Begin by preparing your layers. Coat the bottom of the crockpot with the bacon pieces and follow with a layer of the sausage. Slice and dice the bell peppers, onions, mushrooms, and spinach, and create layers from there: first bell peppers, then the onions, then the spinach, then the mushrooms. Afterwards, follow with a layer of chopped Feta cheese and a layer of the Monterrey Jack cheese, shredded. To the side, beat all twelve eggs, the heavy cream, and salt and pepper together in a large bowl. Pour the egg and cream overtop the layers.

Cover the crockpot and allow it to cook on low for a full twelve hours prior to serving. Enjoy!

SIMPLE LOW-CARB SAUSAGE AND EGG BREAKFAST

Recipe Makes 12 Servings.
Nutritional Breakdown Per Serving: 252 calories, 2 grams net carbohydrates, 20 grams fat, 16 grams protein.

Ingredients:
12 eggs
12 ounces sausage
¼ cup 2% milk
2 cups Cheddar cheese
Salt and pepper to taste

Directions:
Begin by browning the sausage in a saucepan for about five minutes. To the side, whisk together the eggs, milk and the cheese. Place the sausage on the bottom of the slow cooker, and pour the egg mixture overtop the sausage. Salt and pepper the mixture,

and place the lid on the slow cooker once more.
Allow it to cook on low for five hours. Remove the
casserole and serve warm.

HASH BROWN LOW-CARBOHYDRATE BREAKFAST CASSEROLE

Recipe Makes 12 Servings.
Nutritional Breakdown Per Serving: 320 calories, 8 grams net carbohydrates, 20 grams fat, 25 grams protein.

Ingredients:

½ cup milk
12 eggs
16 breakfast sausages
1 cup onion
1 cup bell pepper
12 ounces frozen hash brown potatoes
2 cups Mozzarella cheese
1.5 cups Parmesan cheese
Salt and pepper to taste

Directions:

Whisk together the milk, eggs, and salt and pepper together in a large bowl. To the side, place the sausages in a skillet and brown them until they are completely cooked. Afterwards, drain the fat into the slow cooker.

Begin by layering one half of the twelve ounces of hash brown potatoes on the bottom of the slow cooker. Afterwards, cover the hash browns with half of the sausages. Layer half of the mozzarella and half of the Parmesan cheese overtop the sausages. Next, repeat the layers: first hash browns, then the sausages, and then the cheeses.

Pour the egg and milk mixture overtop the layered ingredients. Place the cover over the crockpot and allow the eggs to cook on low for a full eight hours. Enjoy!

PORK-BASED LOW-CARBOHYDRATE
SLOW COOKER RECIPES

MAPLE CINNAMON PORK RIBS

Recipe Makes 4 Servings.

Nutritional Breakdown Per Serving: 185 calories, 2 grams net carbohydrates, 10 grams fat, 22 grams protein.

Ingredients:

¼ tsp. cinnamon

¼ tsp. allspice

¼ cup onion

2 pounds pork ribs

½ tsp. garlic powder

¼ tsp. ginger

1 tbsp. sugar-free maple syrup

1 tsp. pepper

1 tbsp. soy sauce

Directions:

Bring the cinnamon, the allspice, the chopped onion, the garlic powder, the ginger, the maple syrup, the pepper, and the soy sauce together in a medium-sized bowl and stir well.

To the side, place the ribs into the crockpot and pour the mixture overtop the ribs. Cover the crockpot and cook the ribs on low for about eight hours. The ribs should be tender.

PORK TENDERLOIN SPIKED WITH PAPRIKA

Recipe Makes 6 Servings.
Nutritional Breakdown Per Serving: 160 calories, 2.4 grams net carbohydrates, 8.2 grams fat, 22 grams protein.

Ingredients:
1 cup chicken stock
1.5 pounds pork tenderloin
2 tbsp. smoked paprika
½ cup salsa—spicy or not, your choice
Salt and pepper to taste
1 tbsp. oregano

Directions:
Pour the salsa, the chicken stock, the oregano, the paprika, and a few shakes of the salt and pepper together in a small bowl. Stir well.

Afterwards, trim the fat from the pork tenderloins and place the pork in the slow cooker. Pour the prepared sauce from the small bowl over the tenderloin and allow the tenderloin to cook for a full four hours on a high setting. Make sure the lid is on the crockpot the entire time. Afterwards, remove the top and shred the pork with a few large knives or forks. Cook the pork for an additional twenty minutes, this time with the top off. Serve overtop salad greens and with a side of vegetables for a delicious, vibrant meal.

SLOW COOKER LATIN AMERICAN PORK ADOBADO

Recipe Makes 8 Servings.
Nutritional Breakdown Per Serving: 165 calories, 4.1 grams net carbohydrates, 7 grams fat, 24 grams protein.

Ingredients:
3 ounces New Mexico Chilies, dried
3 pounds pork shoulder
6 cloves of garlic
2 chipotles
1 tbsp. coriander
1 onion
1 tsp. oregano
1 tsp. cumin
Salt and pepper to taste
2 bay leaves

Directions:

Place the New Mexico chilies in a pan and sauté for five minutes on medium-high heat. The chilies should begin to puff to release their flavor. Afterwards, remove the seeds and the stem from the chilies.

Place the chilies in a small pot and fill the pot with water, completely covering the peppers. Bring the water to a boil and allow the water to simmer for a full five minutes. Afterwards, turn the heat off and let the chilies rest in the hot water for thirty minutes.

Next, remove the chili peppers from the water with an additional one cup of the water in the pot. Pour the water and chilies into a blender along with the chipotles, the coriander, the cumin, the oregano, the garlic, and the onion. Blend until the mixture is completely combined. This creation in your blender is the adobo sauce.

Afterwards, cut the fat from the pork shoulder and season the pork shoulder with salt and pepper. Pour a bit of the adobo sauce to line the very bottom of the slow cooker prior to placing the pork shoulder on the bottom of the slow cooker. Pour the remaining adobo sauce on top of the pork. Also, add the bay leaves.

Allow the pork to cook for eight hours on medium-low heat. The pork should be tender. After eight hours, pull the pork apart to formulate "strings" and stir the strings to completely coat with the adobo sauce. Remove the bay leaves prior to serving. Serve the pork adobo on its own or over a few leafy greens.

THREE-INGREDIENT SLOW COOKER PORK CHOPS

Recipe Makes 10 Servings.
Nutritional Breakdown Per Serving: 235 calories, 8 grams net carbohydrates, 12 grams fat, 21 grams protein.

Ingredients:
10 pork chops
1 can cream of mushroom soup
½ cup ketchup (low sugar)

Directions:
Place each pork chop at the bottom of the crockpot. To the side, mix together the ketchup and the cream of mushroom soup. Pour the mixture over the pork chops and cover the crockpot with the top. Cook the pork on a low setting for nine hours prior to serving. Note: Cream of mushroom soup and ketchup are absolutely a strange combination; however, it's a combination not to be missed.

SPICY PORK COCHINITA PIBIL

Recipe Makes 8 Servings.
Nutritional Breakdown Per Serving: 165 calories, 4 grams net carbohydrates, 7 grams fat, 24 grams protein.

Ingredients:

3 pounds pork shoulder
2 habaneros
½ cup orange juice
1 onion
3 garlic cloves
1 tbsp. coriander
1 tsp. dried oregano
1 tsp. cumin
½ cup chicken broth
4 tbsp. Achiote paste
½ cup apple cider vinegar
Salt and pepper to taste

Directions:

Begin by preparing both the pork shoulder and the vegetables. Trim the fat from the pork shoulder, and dice the habanero, the garlic cloves, and the onion.

Next, prepare the pork shoulder by salting and peppering it. Rub the pork with the Achiote paste, as well.

Place a layer of onions and garlic on the bottom of the slow cooker. Layer the pork shoulder overtop the onions and garlic.

To the side, combine the rest of the ingredients in a small bowl: the ½ cup orange juice, the coriander, the dried oregano, the cumin, the chicken broth, and the apple cider vinegar. Pour this over the pork shoulder, and place the slow cooker top back on.

Heat the pork on a low setting for eight hours. After eight hours, pull the pork apart with two large forks to combine the sauce with all of its pieces. Enjoy over greens, on its own, or between two pieces of low-carbohydrate bread.

BALSAMIC SLOW COOKER PORK ROAST

Recipe Makes 8 Servings.
Nutritional Breakdown Per Serving: 215 calories, 4 grams net carbohydrates, 12 grams fat, 21 grams protein.

Ingredients:

2 pounds pork shoulder, boneless
½ tsp. garlic powder
1/3 cup chicken broth
½ tsp. red pepper flakes
1 tbsp. Worcestershire sauce
1/3 cup balsamic vinegar
1 tbsp. honey
Salt and pepper

Directions:

Completely coat the pork shoulder with garlic powder, salt, and red pepper flakes. Place the pork in the slow cooker. To the side, mix together the balsamic vinegar and the broth. Pour the mixture over the pork. Afterwards, pour the honey over the pork as well.

Place the lid on the slow cooker, and heat the pork to a low setting. Allow it to cook for a full eight hours. Enjoy!

Recipe Makes 12 Servings.
Nutritional Breakdown Per Serving: 260 calories,
1 gram net carbohydrate, 16 grams fat, 20 grams
protein.

BBQ sauce Ingredients:
¼ cup yellow mustard
½ tsp. allspice
3 tbsp. apple cider vinegar
2 tsp. hot sauce
3 tbsp. ketchup (low sugar)
½ tsp. xanthan gum
2 tbsp. sugar substitute

Pulled Pork Ingredients:
3 pounds pork shoulder, boneless
1 tsp. garlic powder
1 tsp. onion powder
1 tsp. kosher salt

½ tsp. paprika

½ tsp. black pepper

½ tsp. celery salt

½ tsp. ground allspice

½ tsp. mustard powder

1/8 tsp. ground cloves

½ cup water

Pulled Pork Directions:

Bring together the garlic powder, the onion powder, the pepper, the salt, the paprika, the allspice, the celery salt, the cloves, and the mustard powder. Stir well and rub the mixture over the pork shoulder.

Next, pour the water into the slow cooker. Place the pork in the slow cooker and put the lid overtop. Cook the pork on a high setting for a full four hours. The pulled pork should be falling apart. While the meat remains in the slow cooker, shred it with two large forks to assimilate it with the juices.

BBQ Sauce Directions:

After you remove the pork from the slow cooker, skim out the fat and solids from the slow cooker. Throw them away. Next, add the sauce ingredients to the slow cooker and whisk well. Place the lid back on the slow cooker and allow the sauce to cook on a high setting for ten minutes.

Place the meat back in the slow cooker and stir the meat until it's completely coated with the BBQ sauce. Serve warm.

BEEF-BASED LOW-CARBOHYDRATE
SLOW COOKER RECIPES

COFFEE AND BROWN SUGAR-BRAISED BRISKET

Recipe Makes 8 Servings.
Nutritional Breakdown Per Serving: 225 calories, 8 grams net carbohydrates, 8 grams fat, 32 grams protein.

Ingredients:

1 tbsp. ground coffee

2 tbsp. brown sugar

1 tsp. garlic powder

1 tbsp. paprika

1 tsp. salt

1 tsp. pepper

2 onions

3 pounds boneless beef brisket

1 tbsp. balsamic vinegar

½ cup coffee

Directions:

To begin, bring together ground coffee, brown sugar, garlic powder, paprika, salt, and pepper in a small bowl. Stir well.

To the side, trim the fat from the 3 pounds of brisket and coat the surface of the brisket with the prepared mixture. If you must cut the brisket to fit it in the slow cooker, do so now and rub the interior parts with the mixture, as well.

Place the meat in the slow cooker and slice the onions to the side. Place the onion slices alongside the brisket.

To the side, bring together the vinegar and the half cup of coffee. Stir and pour the mixture over the brisket. Place the cover on the slow cooker and place the slow cooker on low heat. Allow the brisket to cook for a full nine hours. Serve the brisket with a side of the onion slices. Enjoy!

THAI AND CURRY FOUR-HOUR GROUND BEEF

Recipe Makes 4 Servings.
Nutritional Breakdown Per Serving: 223 calories, 8 grams net carbohydrates, 8 grams fat, 25 grams protein.

Ingredients:
1 leek
1 pound ground beef
1 tsp. ginger
2 garlic cloves
1 tbsp. red curry paste
1 tsp. lime zest
1 ½ cups tomato sauce
½ cup coconut milk
1 tbsp. soy sauce
2 tsp. lime juice

Directions:
Place the ground beef in a saucepan and brown it a bit over medium heat. While it browns, slice the leek and mince both the ginger and the cloves.

Once the ground beef has browned, place it in the crockpot along with the garlic, the leek, the red curry paste, the ginger, the tomato sauce, the lime zest, and the soy sauce. Place the cover over the crockpot and allow the beef to cook for a full four hours on low heat. Afterwards, remove the pot lid and pour in the lime juice and the coconut milk. Stir well. Allow the beef to cook for an additional fifteen minutes without the top on, and serve it alone or with a side of vegetables.

BEEF-STUFFED GREEN PEPPERS

Recipe Makes 5 Servings.
Nutritional Breakdown Per Serving: 220 calories, 7 grams net carbohydrates, 15 grams fat, 13 grams protein.

Ingredients:
5 green peppers
1 cup grated cauliflower
1 ½ pounds ground beef
½ cup salsa
½ cup unsalted walnuts
1 egg
Salt and pepper to taste
1 cup shredded sharp cheddar cheese

Directions:
Begin by slicing the very top of your peppers off. Completely remove all the seeds, but place the tops to the side. You'll need them later.

To the side, mix together the grated cauliflower, the ground beef, the salsa, the walnuts, the egg, the salt and pepper, and the cheese. Stir well and divide it into each green pepper as stuffing.

Place each stuffed pepper into the slow cooker and add about one or two inches of water to the bottom of the crockpot. Place the tops of the peppers back on the peppers, and place the top of the slow cooker back on the slow cooker. Heat the crockpot to the lowest setting and cook the peppers for eight hours. Enjoy!

SLOW COOKER PHILLY CHEESESTEAK

Recipe Makes 4 Servings.
Nutritional Breakdown Per Serving: 210 calories, 5 grams net carbohydrates, 14 grams fat, 21 grams protein.

Ingredients:
1 ½ pounds sliced beefsteak
¾ cup onion
1 green pepper
32 ounces beef broth
8 ounces mushrooms

Directions:
Begin by preparing your ingredients. Slice the onion, green pepper, and the mushrooms. Add the vegetables to the slow cooker. Afterwards, slice the beefsteak and add the steak to the slow cooker. Pour the beef broth overtop the steak and allow the slow cooker to cook the ingredients for eight hours on a low temperature.

Afterwards, drain the vegetables and the meat and sauté them a bit in a saucepan with a tablespoon of butter. Eat the Philly steak over greens or with low carbohydrate bread for a scrumptious feast.

BEEF SAUCE AND SPAGHETTI SQUASH

Recipe Makes 6 Servings.
Nutritional Breakdown Per Serving: 90 calories, 6 grams net carbohydrates, 8 grams fat, 9 grams protein.

Ingredients:
1 ¼ pound ground beef
1 ½ cup chicken stock
½ cup onion
1 tbsp. parsley
3 tbsp. tomato paste
1 tsp. fennel powder
1 tsp. garlic powder
¼ tsp. pepper
1/8 tsp. salt
1 spaghetti squash

Directions:
Begin by bringing the ground beef into a large pot and browning it a bit on medium-high heat. After it browns, drain the remaining grease from the saucepan into the slow cooker.

To the side, prepare your vegetables. Slice and dice the onion and chop your parsley, if using fresh parsley. Note: you can utilize dried parsley as well.

Toss the onions into the saucepan in which the meat is still browning. Allow the onions to soften. Next, toss in the chicken stock and tomato paste to the meat and onions. Stir well for two minutes.

Next, add everything to the slow cooker. Pour the beef, tomato and onion mixture into the slow cooker along with the garlic powder, the fennel powder, and the salt and pepper.

Cut the spaghetti squash in half and completely remove the seeds. Place the squash upside down in the slow cooker.

Place the top on the slow cooker and cook the sauce and spaghetti squash on a low setting for a full five hours.

Afterwards, remove the spaghetti squash carefully and utilize a fork to pull out the spaghetti squash strands. Pour the meat sauce overtop the spaghetti squash, and enjoy.

EGGPLANT AND PARMESAN BOLOGNESE

Recipe Makes 8 Servings.
Nutritional Breakdown Per Serving: 145 calories, 8 grams net carbohydrates, 6 grams fat, 15 grams protein.

Ingredients:
1 pound ground beef
6 garlic cloves
1 onion
8 cups chopped eggplant
28 ounce can crushed tomatoes
½ cup chicken broth
½ cup Parmesan cheese
2 bay leaves
Salt and pepper

Directions:
Begin by preparing the vegetables. Slice and dice the onions, the garlic cloves, and the eggplant. Next, place the ground beef, the onion, the garlic, and a bit of salt and pepper in a saucepan and cook over medium heat until the meat and vegetables have browned.

Pour the saucepan ingredients into the slow cooker. Add the chicken broth, the tomatoes, the Parmesan, and the bay leaves to the slow cooker, as well. Next, add the eight cups of chopped eggplant. Stir well.

Place the cover on the slow cooker and heat the slow cooker on low. Allow it to cook for eight hours. The eggplant should be completely broken down into a sort of cream. Enjoy your Eggplant and Parmesan Bolognese!

CHICKEN-BASED LOW-CARBOHYDRATE
SLOW COOKER RECIPES

BUTTERED CHICKEN MAKHANI

Recipe Makes 6 Servings.
Nutritional Breakdown Per Serving: 240 calories,
5 grams net carbohydrates, 13 grams fat, 24 grams
protein.

Ingredients:

2 pounds chicken breast

1 shallot

1 tbsp. vegetable oil

2 tbsp. butter

¼ white onion

2 tsp. lemon juice

1 inch ginger

4 garlic cloves

1 tsp. chili powder

2 tsp. garam masala

1 bay leaf

1 tsp. ground cumin

¼ cup half and half
¼ cup plain yogurt
¾ cup 2% milk
1 cup tomato sauce
2 ¼ tsp. cayenne pepper
Salt and pepper to taste

Directions:

Begin by preparing your vegetables. Slice and dice the shallot, the onion, the garlic cloves, and the ginger.

Next, toss the shallot and the onion in 1 tbsp. of vegetable oil in a medium-sized saucepan. Heat the vegetables on a medium heat, and allow the shallot and the onion to soften.

Next, add the lemon juice, the ginger, the butter, the garlic, the chili powder, the garam masala, the cumin, the cayenne, and the bay leaf. Cook for an additional minute; you should be able to smell the spices. Next, add the tomato sauce. Cook for an additional two minutes, and make sure to continue to stir.

Pour the milk, half and half, and yogurt into the mixture as well. Next, reduce the heat to a low setting. Continue to stir for an additional ten minutes.

Pour the entire mixture into a blender and blend well until the ingredients are combined.

To the side, cut the chicken breast into bit-sized pieces and add the pieces to the slow cooker. Pour the green mixture overtop the chicken and allow it to cook on a low setting for four hours. Afterwards, serve warm.

CHIPOTLE CHICKEN BARBACOA

Recipe Makes 6 Servings.
Nutritional Breakdown Per Serving: 208 calories, 4 grams net carbohydrates, 5 grams fat, 34 grams protein.

Ingredients:
2 pounds of chicken breast
7 ounces of chipotles in adobo sauce (easy to find in a can at any grocery)
1 onion
4 garlic cloves
1 tsp. oregano
½ tbsp. cumin
½ cup chicken broth
Salt and pepper to taste

Directions:
To begin, salt and pepper the chicken breasts. Place each of the chicken breasts inside the crockpot.

Quarter the onion, and place the onions inside the crockpot along with the garlic cloves.

To the side, stir together the cumin, oregano, chicken broth, and the chipotles in adobo sauce. Remember to leave the chipotles completely whole.

Cover the slow cooker and set the heat to high. Allow the chicken to cook for a full four hours. Afterwards, remove the garlic, the whole chipotles, and the onions and shred the chicken utilizing to big forks. Serve and enjoy!

CHICKEN CROCKPOT MID-DAY CHOWDER

Recipe Makes 9 Servings.
Nutritional Breakdown Per Serving: 116 calories, 9 grams net carbohydrates, 7 grams fat, 3 grams protein.

Ingredients:

1 can yellow corn
1 can Cream of Chicken soup
1 can cheddar cheese dip
1 pound skinless, boneless chicken breast
½ cup green chilies
1 can chicken broth
1 cup sour cream

Directions:

Bring the cream of chicken soup, the corn, the chicken broth, and the green chilies together in the slow cooker. Stir well. To the side, chop the skinless, boneless chicken into bite sized pieces. Add the chicken to the crockpot, and put the crockpot on a low heat setting. Cook the soup for a full four hours.

Afterwards, mix the sour cream and cheese dip into the crockpot. Cook for an additional ten minutes. Serve warm.

GREEN CURRY CHICKEN DINNER

Recipe Makes 8 Servings.
Nutritional Breakdown Per Serving: 240 calories, 5.5 grams net carbohydrates, 10 grams fat, 35 grams protein.

Ingredients:

2 ½ pounds chicken breast

1 red pepper

1 onion

1 cup broccoli

1 ½ can coconut milk

3 tbsp. green curry paste

4 garlic cloves

3 tbsp. brown sugar

1 can of mini corn

2 tbsp. cornstarch

Directions:

Begin by preparing your vegetables. Chop the onion, red peppers, and the broccoli. Furthermore, mince the garlic cloves completely.

Next, pour the coconut milk, the brown sugar, the green curry paste, and the garlic into the slow cooker. Whisk the ingredients together in the slow cooker.

Add the vegetables: red pepper, onion, and broccoli. Also, cut the chicken breast into bite-sized pieces and add the chicken breast to the slow cooker.

Place the slow cooker on a low heat setting and allow it to cook for four hours. After four hours have passed, whisk together 2 tbsp. of water and the 2 tbsp. of cornstarch. Pour this mixture into the crockpot and stir briefly. Allow the curry to thicken via this cornstarch for an additional thirty minutes on the lowest setting. Enjoy.

ARTICHOKE AND FETA-STUFFED CHICKEN BREASTS

Recipe Makes 6 Servings.
Nutritional Breakdown Per Serving: 205 calories, 4 grams net carbohydrates, 5 grams fat, 34 grams protein.

Ingredients:

2 pounds skinless, boneless chicken breast
2 cups red peppers
3 cups spinach
1 cup artichoke hearts
¼ cup black olives
4 ounces feta cheese
1 tsp. garlic powder
1 tbsp. oregano
1 ½ cups chicken broth
Salt and pepper to taste

Direction:

Begin by preparing the vegetables. Chop the red peppers and roast them in the oven for thirty minutes or, alternately, brown them a bit in a saucepan with a tsp. of olive oil. Afterwards, slice the black olives, slice and dice the artichoke hearts, chop up the oregano, and chop the spinach.

After you've prepared the vegetable filling, mix together the roasted red peppers, the artichoke hearts, the spinach, the feta cheese, the garlic, and the oregano in a medium-sized bowl. Stir well.

To the side, salt and pepper the chicken breasts and then make a deep cut in the very center of the top of the chicken breast. You're trying to make a sort of pocket. Do not cut all the way through the chicken.

Next, stuff the chicken with the vegetable and cheese mixture. Place each piece of chicken in the slow cooker. In order to allow each chicken to fit, you might have to face each pocket "up" in the slow cooker. This further allows the filling to stay in the chicken.

Next, add the chicken broth and place the slow cooker's cover on top. Heat the crock pot on a low setting and cook for four hours. Make sure the chicken is cooked all the way through prior to serving. Enjoy!

JAMAICAN JERK CHICKEN

Recipe Makes 12 Servings.
Nutritional Breakdown Per Serving: 106 calories, 1.8 grams net carbohydrates, 2 grams fat, 18 grams protein.

Ingredients:

1 ½ pound skinless chicken breasts (with bone)
1 ½ pound skinless, boneless chicken thigh
4 garlic cloves
¼ cup lime juice
1 tbsp. dark brown sugar
1 tbsp. fresh ginger
4 scallions
2 tsp. allspice berries
4 habanero peppers
2 tbsp. white vinegar
1 red pepper
Salt and pepper to taste

Directions:

Begin by placing the chicken in the crockpot.

To the side, add the lime juice, the garlic cloves, the brown sugar, the ginger, the scallions, the allspice berries, the habanero peppers, the white vinegar, and the red pepper to a blender. Note: you might want to add the habanero peppers one at a time to achieve the right level of heat.

Pour the blended ingredients overtop the chicken and place the lid back on the slow cooker. Cook the chicken on medium-low heat for a full six hours.

Afterwards, shred the chicken in the slow cooker to assimilate all the ingredients into the meat. Enjoy!

CHILI AND SOUP LOW-CARBOHYDRATE
SLOW COOKER RECIPES

BLACK BEANS AND CHICKEN CHILI LOW-CARBOHYDRATE RECIPE

Recipe Makes 10 Servings.
Nutritional Breakdown Per Serving: 150 calories, 9 grams net carbohydrates, 4 grams fat, 16 grams protein.

Ingredients:
3 entire skinless and boneless chicken breasts
1 onion
2 sweet red peppers
4 ounces green chilies
3 tbsp. olive oil
2 tsp. cumin
2 tbsp. chili powder
1 tsp. coriander
1 can Italian-stewed tomatoes
2 cans black beans
1 cup chicken broth

Directions:
To begin, cube the chicken breasts and slice and dice all the vegetables: the red peppers, the green chilies, and the onion. Place the cubed chicken, chilies, onion, and the red peppers in olive oil heated in the saucepan and sauté until the chicken holds no pink coloring. Next, add the chili powder, garlic, cumin, and the coriander. Cook for one additional minute.

Pour this entire mixture into a crockpot and add the rinsed beans, tomatoes, and the chicken broth. Stir well and cover the crockpot. Place the crockpot on low and allow it to cook for a full five hours.

Salt and pepper to taste, and enjoy this low-carbohydrate chicken chili on a cold autumn evening!

SLOW COOKER SPICY CHICKEN SOUP

Recipe Makes 8 Servings.
Nutritional Breakdown Per Serving: 225 calories, 9.5 grams net carbohydrates, 13 grams fat, 17 grams protein.

Ingredients:

3 chicken breasts
4 cups of water
¼ cabbage
½ onion
1 cup salsa
1 can tomatoes
18 ounces cream cheese
1 tbsp. garlic salt
4 tbsp. heavy whipping cream
1 tbsp. cumin
Salt and pepper to taste

Directions:

Begin by bringing the whole chicken breasts, chopped onion, and the shredded cabbage together in the crockpot. Add four cups of water. Cook the mixture on high for four hours or on low for eight hours. The chicken should be done.

Afterwards, remove the chicken carefully and shred it into small, easy-to-manage pieces. Return the chicken pieces to the pot and add everything else to the crockpot: salsa, tomatoes, cream cheese, garlic salt, whipping cream, cumin, and salt and pepper to taste. Cook the mixture until the cream cheese is completely melted. The soup should be creamy. Serve hot!

LOW CARB SLOW COOKER MINESTRONE ALL-VEGGIE SOUP

Recipe Makes 11 Servings.
Nutritional Breakdown Per Serving: 115 calories, 4 grams net carbohydrates, 3 grams fat, 3 grams protein.

Ingredients:
3 cloves garlic
1 onion
2 cups celery
¼ cup parsley
2 cups green beans
1 cup broccoli
2 cups cauliflower
2 cups zucchini squash
Fresh basil
Fresh sage
5 cups water

Directions:
Begin by preparing the vegetables. Chop garlic, onion, parsley, celery, broccoli, green beans, zucchini, and the cauliflower. Add all the vegetables to your slow cooker. Pour in the five cups of water, as well. Set the heat on the slow cooker to low, and allow the vegetables to cook for eight hours.

After the vegetables are tender, remove two cups of the vegetables from the crockpot. Pour the vegetables into a blender and puree them until they are completely blended. Add the pureed vegetables back to the slow cooker. Serve warm. Enjoy this hearty delight!

BEER AND CHOCOLATE LOW CARBOHYDRATE PORK CHILI

This chili takes miniscule amounts of chocolate and beer—two very anti-diet ingredients! However, the chocolate adds a rich color to the chili, and the beer provides ample flavor. All in all, this recipe lends only 6 net carbohydrates per serving!

Recipe Makes 12 Servings.
Nutritional Breakdown Per Serving: 315 calories, 6 grams net carbohydrates, 19 grams fat, 27 grams protein.

Ingredients:
1 pound pork meat
3 pounds beef
4 tbsp. canola oil
1/3 cup chili powder
1 celery rib
1 onion
1 tbsp. green chilies
3 garlic cloves
¾ cup beer
32 ounces beef broth
2 tbsp. dark chocolate
¾ cup tomato sauce
1 tsp. dried oregano
3 tsp. cumin
½ tsp. mustard

½ tsp. salt

½ tsp. cayenne pepper

Directions:

Begin by sprinkling the chili powder overtop the pork meat and the beef meat. Cut the meat into smaller, bite-sized cubes, and sprinkle a bit more. Utilize half of the chili powder in this step. Next, place the cubed bits of meat into a saucepan and brown it in 2 tbsp. of the canola oil. After it's browned, drain the meat and set it to the side. Next, place the chopped onion and celery into the remaining oil. Sauté the vegetables until they're a bit crispy. Next, add minced garlic, the minced chilies, and the rest of the chill powder. Cook for an additional minute.

Next, pour the vegetable mixture into the crockpot and add the sautéed meat. Stir in the beef broth, tomato sauce, beer, cumin, chocolate, mustard, oregano, salt, and the cayenne. Cover the crockpot and allow the chili to cook on low heat for a full six hours. The meat should be completely tender. Enjoy your low-carbohydrate, steaming chili.

CHICKEN PARMESAN SLOW COOKER SOUP

Recipe Makes 4 Servings.
Nutritional Breakdown Per Serving: 175 calories, 4 grams net carbohydrates, 10 grams fat, 12 grams protein.

Ingredients:
½ tsp. salt
1/8 tsp. pepper
1 cup water
1 cup zucchini
1 onion
2 celery stalks
1/8 cup parsley
1 tsp. beef stock
½ tsp. poultry seasoning
1 skinless, boneless chicken breast
¼ tsp. nutmeg
1/3 cup parmesan cheese

Directions:
Bring the salt, pepper, water, zucchini, onion, celery stalks, parsley, beef stock, and poultry seasoning together in your slow cooker. Cover the slow cooker and heat the interior mixture on a low setting for five hours. Afterwards, dice the chicken and add the chicken to the mixture along with the nutmeg. Cover the crockpot and cook for one more hour. The chicken should be tender.

Next, remove the top from the crockpot and pour in the grated Parmesan cheese. Stir as it melts and assimilates into the soup. Season with salt and pepper as you please!

SLOW COOKER MEATBALL STEW

This recipe calls for low-carbohydrate meatballs.
The meatball recipe is outlined below along with the
stew recipe.

Stew Recipe Makes 9 Servings.
Nutritional Breakdown Per Serving: 119 calories,
5 grams net carbohydrates, 10 grams fat, 14 grams
protein.

Low Carb Baked Meatball Ingredients:
10 ounces spinach
3 pounds ground beef
1 cup Parmesan cheese
1 tsp. pepper
2 tsp. salt
2 tsp. basil
2 eggs
2 tsp. Italian seasoning
2 tsp. parsley

2 tsp. garlic powder

Directions:

Begin by preheating the oven to four hundred degrees Fahrenheit. Next, bring together the ground meat, the cheese, the spinach, the eggs, and the spices in a large mixing bowl. Mix well with clean hands. Afterwards, roll the spiced meat into small balls. Think of them as small golf balls. Place the meatballs evenly on a baking sheet, and bake the meatballs for a full fifteen minutes. Remove the meatballs and flip them onto the other side. Return the baking sheet to the oven and cook for ten more minutes.

Note: These meatballs add a trace amount of carbohydrates to the overall stew. Look to the stew ingredients and recipe below.

Stew Ingredients:

1 carrot

3 cups cabbage

1 onion

16 ounces tomatoes

4 celery stalks

2 tbsp. tomato paste

3 cups beef stock

10 meatballs

2 cups spinach

Salt and pepper to taste

Directions:

Begin by preparing your vegetables. Chop the carrot, the cabbage, the onion, the celery stalks, and the tomatoes. Add the vegetables to the slow cooker along with the tomato paste and the beef stock. Salt and pepper the mixture and cook the mixture in the slow cooker on a high heat setting for four hours. Afterwards, add the spinach. To the side, quarter each of your prepared meatballs and place them in the slow cooker. Cook for an additional one hour on high heat prior to serving. Enjoy with a bit of Parmesan cheese garnish.

CREAMY ZUCCHINI SOUP

Recipe Makes 4 Servings.
Nutritional Breakdown Per Serving: 79 calories, 4 grams net carbohydrates, 5 grams fat, 3 grams protein.

Ingredients:
4 cups green zucchini squash
2 cups chicken broth
1 tbsp. butter
½ cup onion
Salt and pepper to taste

Directions:
Begin by chopping the zucchini squash and the onion to formulate four cups of zucchini and a half a cup of onion. Add the vegetables to the slow cooker. Next, add the chicken broth and the butter. Salt and pepper the mixture a bit, and place the top back on your slow cooker. Heat the soup on a low setting for five hours. The zucchini should be tender.

Afterwards, take the soup from the slow cooker and completely blend it in a blender. The texture should be thick and creamy. Enjoy!

KALE, SPINACH, AND ARTICHOKE DIP

Recipe Makes 20 Servings.
Nutritional Breakdown Per Serving: 82 calories, 5 grams net carbohydrates, 4 grams fat, 6.4 grams protein.

Ingredients:
½ onion
3 garlic cloves
28 ounces artichoke hearts (canned)
10 ounces kale
10 ounces spinach
1 cup Mozzarella cheese
1 cup Parmesan cheese
¾ cup sour cream
1 cup Greek yogurt
¼ cup mayonnaise
Salt and pepper to taste

Directions:

Begin by placing the garlic, artichoke hearts, and onion in a food processor. Crunch the vegetables into small pieces.

Next, pour the vegetables into the slow cooker. To the side, chop up the kale and the spinach. Add the kale and spinach to the slow cooker along with the Mozzarella cheese, Parmesan cheese, Greek yogurt, sour cream, and the mayonnaise. Stir the ingredients well.

Place the lid on the slow cooker and cook the dip for four hours on a high setting. Serve warm and season with a bit of salt and pepper. Enjoy with your favourite veggie sticks

Conclusion

Low Carb Slow Cooker Cookbook lends you 30 easy, flavorful recipes to supercharge your diet plan and assimilate taste and flavor into your life once more. Look to the spicy chicken soup for a chilly evening; find the eggplant bolognaise waiting for you after a long day at the office; reach for the BBQ pulled pork on a breezy summer day. Each recipe is unique in its creation, and each brings less than 10 net grams of carbohydrates. Your blood sugar level doesn't creep up, and your sugar cravings will decrease endlessly, leaving you wanting healthful, rejuvenating food in the future. Each meal allows your body to enter into ketosis as it burns countless more calories to alter the protein and fat to meet your cell glucose needs. Find health, a slimmer waistline, and much more time in your schedule with the assistance of these thirty recipes. Reap the rewards of the low-carb lifestyle!

Made in the USA
Lexington, KY
05 January 2015